MY MONTH IN HELL

Combat In Sarajevo

JAMES (DAN) WRIGHT

outskirts press

My Month in Hell
Combat In Sarajevo

v1.0

Outskirts Press, Inc.
http://www.outskirtspress.com

ISBN: 978-1-9772-3067-6

PRINTED IN THE UNITED STATES OF AMERICA

"Tear down this wall", also known as the Berlin Wall Speech, is a speech delivered by U.S. President Ronald Reagan in West Berlin on Friday, June 12, 1987.

STARTED EVERYTHING!

WHILE I WAS in High School. Russia did tear down the Berlin Wall, which was constructed at the end of WWII. Finally allowing East and West Germany to reunite with each other. This caused a Revolution in Russia. A lot of the Russian military wanted to remain in control over the people. The Revolution did not last long. Within a couple of years, a Russian territory known as Yugoslavia split apart. Well part of this territory is a country called Bosnia. Bosnia had a mixture of cultures and religions. They formed a government with similarities to the United States. Not the same but closer to it then old school Russia. Was not long till trouble started. In that area were Russian trained troops who wanted life to return to the old ways. They were called Serbs. They attached the Bosnian capitol in Sarajevo. The UN sent troops to the region to assist the Bosnian government in regaining order in the region.

Meanwhile back in the USA I graduated from Patapsco High School, already married and a father. In the beginning of my 12th grade year of school I got my girlfriend pregnant. So, I asked her to marry me. We were married on April 10, 1990 and she gave birth to our son June 2nd, 1990. I graduated the next day June 3rd. I worked at

Overnite Transportation in Elkridge Md but was laid off the following January 1991. They were making cutbacks and I did not have enough time in. At that time Saddam Hussein had already invaded Kuwait and the US military was in Saudi Arabia preparing to remove Iraq from Kuwait. It was called Operation Desert Shield. Jobs were kind of scarce and hard to find in the early nineties. I needed a good paying job to support my family, so I joined the Army. While I was in basic training the activity in the Middle East got physical. This was called Operation Desert Storm. Iraq who had the 4th largest Army in the world did not last long against the United States. The war was over before I finished basic training.

Basic training was a little tough on me. See I knew I had acute arthritis in both of my knees since I was about 13. Still I did not mention that fact to the military when I joined. I was supposed to go to Jump School after Basic And AIT, and be stationed at Ft Brag in North Carolina with the 82nd Airborne. Majority of all the exercises we performed in Basic training were no problem for me, I actually did very well in Basic except for the running. Despite the fact I have smoked since I was 7, breathing was not the problem, it was always my knees. Sometimes they would swell up twice their size, but I dealt with the pain and did not slow down. I did very well at the range too with the M16. First two times we went to the range, we shot at paper targets. I shot expert both times, but the targets were only about fifty yards away. The next time we shot at pop-up targets, which looked like people silhouettes. They would pop up for three seconds and go back down, anywhere between twenty-five to three hundred feet away. First time I shot at this range I hit thirty-eight out of forty. During Basic you only sleep for a few hours a night, so you are always tired. The day before going to the range for the second time, I slept when I was supposed to be cleaning my M16. I found out why you keep your weapon clean. We went to the range and my M16 jammed after the first fifteen rounds. By the time I cleared it and started shooting I had already missed several targets by clearing the jam. I only shot twenty-five out of forty. Which sucked, but I made up for it by the third time we went to the range, I hit forty out of forty. After Basic was over I went to AIT to learn my job as a Diesel Mechanic. I learned that very quickly, because I had worked on cars most of my life helping my dad. I became a squad leader and also was promoted to E-2 during AIT. About halfway through my training, my knees got the better of me. The drill instructor saw my knee was swelled up and sent me to get it checked out by the doctor. They did their tests and they told me I had acute arthritis in my knees, and I acted shocked. The doctor was a Colonel and he told me that I cannot go to Jump School, because of my knees. He said even if you land correctly; you have a chance of not ever walking anymore. He ordered me to drop Jump School, so I did. About three days after I dropped Jump School, I received a letter from the Army. It stated that I broke the contract with the Military by dropping Jump School, and they would send me to where they wanted to. See when I joined the Army, I got to choose my first duty station, and did not want to go overseas. So just before my training was over; I received orders to go to Germany, so I went.

After all my training was over, I was sent to Wiesbaden Germany for my first tour of duty. I was a diesel mechanic with the 5/6 Cavalry. It was there that I met the man who would save my life. I was working on a truck when Sergeant Johnson, my platoon Sgt came over and introduced me to a new recruit to our motor pool. His name was Bob, and I walked him around to introduce him to everyone. Him and I got along great together and quickly became best friends. He was a year younger than I was, and he was from Ohio, but he had the appearance of a surfer guy from California. Tall, blonde hair, and blue eyes, I mean if you saw him and did not know him that is what you would think. Everyone said that about him, so it got to be a regular thing that people said "Surfs Up Dude" when Bob was around. He did not mind though; he would smile at it and sometimes hold his arms out like he was surfing. A group of us who worked together went into different German bars and stores, and some even had German girlfriends. We would have cookouts and even watch movies together. They became some of the best friends I ever had. We would talk about people we knew back in the states and where we were from. I would talk about my son Daniel a lot, and they would tell me your too young to have a kid since we were all 19 and 20 years old. 5/6 Cav as it was commonly referred to was disbanded in March of 1992. So, a lot of us were sent to 12th Aviation Brigade on the same base. Our new Captain was a hardcore soldier from a Ranger Unit. His name was Captain Nickles. I will never forget the sirens going off in the barracks around 2am in July of 1992. We quickly got into formation in front of the barracks, and our Captain told all of us that Iraq had started hostel acts again in the Middle East. He said we had two hours to collect our gear, weapon from the Armory and be on the flight line ready to go.

All of us were put into two C-5 airplanes, where we flew to Saudi Arabia Dhahran. We quickly set up a perimeter and camp outside of the city. What was freaking a lot of us out was we had our M16s, but no one handed out any bullets. Now here we are in a foreign desert with a huge Arab city in front of us, thinking we are there to maybe getting into battle with enemy troops. I mean wouldn't you be concerned. Aiming an empty weapon at someone shooting at you is not going to stop them from shooting at you. Day to day we did training exercises, and our regular job duties, and had to pull guard duty sometimes. About a week in the dessert we were told that this was a training exercise. Yeah, a lot of us were pissed about it but what could we do. After we found out it was all a crock of crap, some of us would venture out into the city. We would check out some of the street vendors we would pass, and I actually found a T-shirt that said "Welcome To Bum$#@% Egypt" on it. I HAD TO BUY IT. It had a biker looking guy on it with a sword and it had sleeves, but I did not want sleeves, so I cut them off. I loved it and wore it anytime I had a chance. One day my friend Matt came up to me with a weird looking bowl and said you have to try this man. It was a Saudi made meal, it looked like pieces of some kind of meat, so I tried a piece. It had a weird kind of taste, so I said what the hell did I just eat. Very calmly, like nothing was wrong, he said its camel tongue. I said what did you just say, and he said camel tongue man isn't it good. I called him an @##hole and started spitting the rest out. Didn't throw up or nothing, but the thought of what I had eaten made me feel sick. We all got a laugh out of it, but I still shiver when I think I actually ate a camel's tongue. Don't try it, stick with steak, much better. So, we spent two weeks in the desert before returning to Germany.

Meanwhile in Sarajevo the conflict was getting bad for the UN. The Serbs were killing people and putting the bodies in mass graves. They were also attacking the UN shipments of medical supplies and food for the region. Troops from around the globe were sent to assist the UN. Officially the United States were not sending troops to help, but I know better.

On September 3rd, 1992, the sirens in the barracks went off again around 3am. So again, we all got into formation in front of the barracks, and again our Captain told us what the situation was in Bosnia. We were told to get our gear, our weapons from the armory and report to the flight line. A lot of us were saying here we go again another stupid training exercise, there were 48 of us that were going. Little did we know. On our way to Bosnia a Two Star General got up in front of the plain and told us we were going to see combat and we should prepare ourselves. He also said that the United States government will deny any involvement in Bosnia. We were not supposed to discuss this with anyone. Even today, the United States government will tell you we did not get involved with military action in Bosnia until 1995.

We arrived at a UN base in Sarajevo Bosnia in late evening September 3rd, 1992. We stepped off the plane and saw soldiers from different countries walking around, and some were clean cut like us, and some had full beards. We were all assigned to different company tents or barracks if you will. Where we traded our US military gear for UN gear, because we were not there. I had a lot of my friends from the motor pool in my tent, so it was not too bad at first. While on base you could hear explosions and gun fire off in a distance but not close to our base. Food was not too bad, and they even had a bar. My friends and I had fun first couple of days drinking and playing cards after work. Even won some money from some Canadian soldiers playing cards. Did we cheat? I'll never tell!

On September 6th while working on the trucks at the makeshift motor pool, a Major walked in and started to point at some of us saying you all come with me. So, grease still on our hands we went with him. We went to the medical tent where he told us we were getting a crash course on combat medic, we ALL just looked at our hands. Black with grease but we are being trained as combat medics. They taught us basic field medic stuff like how to stop bleeding or even apply a tourniquet, nothing major. After the quick lesson he told us to have our gear and weapons ready to go at 4am the next morning. None of us could sleep so we drank and played cards. I thought I had a fairly good hand, so I talked Matt into fronting me 50 dollars on a hand. I lost; Matt had a better hand then I did. So, I told him I would pay him that Friday when we get paid.

September 7th, 1992 came, and we were nervous but ready to go. We loaded onto these 5 Ton trucks that were loaded up with food and medical supplies. There were about 20 UN doctors and social workers with 30 of us soldiers. We were there to protect the shipments from the Serbs. The convoy consisted of an A-1 Abrams Tank in the front and in the rear. In between there were 18 5 Ton Trucks. We pulled off the base around 5am heading to some town that had been destroyed by the Serbs. Now these convoys had been getting attacked by the Serbs so we were keeping a close eye on every place that could be used for cover that they may be hiding. About an hour into the trip I heard a loud explosion behind us, so I turned around to see what happened. I saw that the tank in the rear of the convoy had been hit with a rocket and it had smoke coming off of it, but it was still working. Almost at the same time you could hear loud tinging from the trucks from people shooting at us. Did not know where it was coming from, but we all got out of the trucks and headed for cover. I laid down behind a dirt mound with a little grass on it and saw my friend Matt jumping out of the back of one of the trucks. Before his feet hit the ground, he was hit with so many bullets it actually held him against the truck for a few seconds before he fell on the ground dead. From my position I started looking for the enemy when I saw a guy about 200 feet away. He was shooting a few rounds and going back down for cover, then he would pop back up and shoot again. So, I aimed my M16 at his position. As soon as I saw the top of his helmet start to come up, I fired two shots. Now I was not a religious man at that time, but I swear to you I heard my soul Scream NO as I pulled the trigger. Up to that moment I had never shot at another human being before. Shooting at targets and shooting at people are two, way different concepts. I watched as both rounds hit him in the head, and I knew I had killed the first person ever in my life. I kept looking for targets and shot at some more, but I do not know if I killed them or not. That day I know I shot 12 people, but I only know I killed one. Not sure if the other 11 lived or died. All you could hear was gunfire and explosions and you could hear people screaming from pain. It smelled like gunpowder and wood burning. One guy I shot, I saw him get hit by four rounds at least, but I only fired one bullet at him. So, I do not count him as one I killed. Not sure which one of us killed him, but a couple of guys claimed it. This battle only lasted about 15 minutes or so. We had two wounded and three killed, one was my friend Matt. The other two were from different regiments and I never met them, but they were American soldiers. That pissed me off!!! We arrived at our destination about an hour after that. There were Marines and Special Forces already there and we unloaded the supplies and went back to our base. My friends and I drank a toast to our friend Matt, let me say A LOT of toasts. Even though we drank heavily that night I don't think any of us got drunk. I think we were more in shock than anything else.

The next day I woke up just in time to see another convoy leaving the base. They had different soldiers on this run, while we were to report to our regular jobs on base. On the side of the motor pool there were piles of used parts that had been replaced by who worked it before we arrived in Sarajevo. While at the motor pool I saw a bunch of old truck seats stacked up in a pile. So, I told my Platoon Sargent I have an idea to put them to use, and he said what's that. I said hold that thought, and I went into the supply truck and grabbed 2 different size flanges. I came back to him and sat the flanges in front of him. He said what am I looking at here. So, I picked up the smaller flange and pointed at the old seats, and I said mount these to the bottom of the seats. Then I pointed at the bigger flange and said mount this to cab of the trucks. Then I put the smaller flange into the bigger flange and spun it around. I told him we could spot the enemy quicker if we were not looking through little windows. He said you would be exposed up there, and I said we are exposed in the trucks. So, he said he would suggest it to the higher command. Later that day Captain Nickles came to the motor pool and asked me to put one together so he could see it. So, I did, I mounted it to the top of a table. I sat down in it and spun completely around, and I said we would have full 360 degrees movement on these things. He liked the idea and said get some made up. So, my friends and I quickly made about 15 of them and mounted the big flange to 15 truck cabs. The next morning, we put the seats on and tested them while driving around base. Worked very well unless you were driving really fast and the breaks were slammed on. I was thrown onto the hood of the truck and down to the ground before I knew what happened. I was a little sore, but nothing broken. So, we found these metal brackets that were also in a trash pile. Almost like little wedges, and we mounted them between the front part of the seats and the little flange. Now the seats were kind of in a laid-back position, so we tried it again. This time it worked. Even at high speed, and quick stops it jolts you but does not throw you. So, we called for Captain Nickles to come see it. We went through all kind of speeds, slamming on the brakes, and the whole time whoever was in the seat had complete control of which way he wanted to point. Captain Nickles liked it so much, he had supply order a couple hundred more flanges of the same size. He looked at me and said good work Wright.

On the 10th of September we went on another convoy. This time we had fewer soldiers but had some Hummers with mounted 50 calibers on them. Trip went really smooth for a while until we came to town that almost looked like a ghost town to me, because there were no people walking around. Just buildings and all you heard were our engines. Well all 15 5 Tons had our seats on them, and you could see all of them spinning back and forth looking for any movement. I was in one too looking around, but none of us saw anything. Then at the end of this town was a large building almost in the center of the street. It was a concrete building with a lot of doors and windows on it. Once we got close to it, we were getting shot at from every window and doorway, even had some on the roof. Everyone quickly got to cover behind the vehicles. I was behind the wheel of one of the Hummers with the 50-calibers mounted on it. Now for those of you who do not know, let me explain the 50-caliber machine gun to you. It is a belt fed machine gun. Each round is about 6 or 7 inches long, and it does a lot of damage to whatever it hits. It has two vertical handles on the rear of it, and it has two triggers. You cannot shoot this weapon with one hand, because of its safety feature. Both triggers must be pressed in for it to fire. Now just having it loaded will not work. There is a charging handle on the right side that must be pulled all the way back and released before firing this weapon. It is like cocking a gun basically. I watched the E6 Staff Sargent charge the 50-caliber, but before he could fire it. He was shot in the arm and fell off the Hummer onto the ground. I looked at the building and I could see flashes everywhere, but you could not see the people. So, I shot a couple of rounds into a couple of windows with my M16. Then I jumped up into the Hummer dropped my M16 on to the bed, and grabbed the already charged 50 Cal. I pulled both triggers and let loose on this building with 500 rounds before the box emptied out. It was like running 2 jackhammers at the same time, I mean it shakes your whole body, and I could feel the Hummer rocking back and forth. I was shooting that thing at every inch of that building. There were huge chunks of concrete falling to the ground, and every door and window were completely gone as if they were never there before. It created so much dust from the building I could hardly see it anymore. When I got off the Hummer, I could feel my arms moving back and forth like I was still firing the 50 Cal. To this day I do not know if I hit anyone in that building or not, but no one ever fired at us from it again. As far as I know no one entered the building to see, if anyone did, I did not hear about it. We just continued with our journey, but went cautiously around the building, or what was left of it. We arrived at our destination and unloaded the supplies and some of the UN doctors stayed with the military units that were stationed there. We returned to our base; all in all it was a successful mission since we only had one wounded soldier.

The next day September 11th we went on two short missions to the next town over and back, and back and forth with no site of the Serbs anywhere. We got back to base and somehow, we got into an argument with some British soldiers that were also on the base. No one threw any punches, but it seemed like it was heading that way. It was broken up when the Captain called us to formation. We formed up, and they walked away. Captain Nickles said we were going on a 10-mile convoy to another desolated town by the Serbs. Then he says choppers have spotted Serb forces on the route we were taken; they were camped along the route. He ordered us to not stair at them or point your weapons at them as this may start a conflict. I said sir, we are already in a conflict with the enemy. He said if they do not fire at you, then you cannot fire at them, so I said yes sir. Even though I thought that was bullcrap, you do not backtalk an officer. After we were released from formation, we all got something to eat and headed to the bar. Guess who was at the bar, yep, the same British soldiers we almost fought with. We were so pissed at what we were just told by our Captain, we did not even think about the problem with the British. It was obvious we were pissed about something else and some of the

British even came over to talk with us, even bought a few rounds for us. They were some cool guys, and we hung out most of that night.

Now its morning, September 12th, and we are getting our gear ready for the run across enemy territory. When a Hummer pulled into our base that had a UN Colonel in it. He hollered for us to gather round men, so we all walked closer to him. He was saying the same thing that our Captain told us the day before. He said they are in peace talks with the Serbs and any aggression on our part could ruin everything. So, we loaded up into our trucks, and headed out. Did not see any Serbs till about 6 miles out. I was on top of the front 5 Ton truck, and as we came up a steep hill, I saw an enemy tank and some trucks parked on the side of the road, so I hollered Heads Up. We kept the same speed as we drove passed them, and those Basterds just stared at us. Did not attack us though, but we knew we were going to meet them later. When we passed them, I lit up a cigarette because I was pissed. I wanted to shoot them all, I mean these were the guys that killed Matt I thought. We were not supposed to smoke while on top of the trucks because we were the lookouts. I heard Captain Nickles from inside my truck, Wright are you smoking up there, and I said no sir as I put my cigarette out on the roof of the truck. With a mile to go, we started to hear loud tinging on the trucks again. So, we stopped and ran for cover, but as I was running, I saw an enemy grenade land within a couple of feet from me. As soon as I saw it, it exploded, and I felt the hot wind from the blast against my legs. Now the kill range of a grenade is anywhere in 5 feet in all directions. This was within two or three feet from me when it blew. Thinking I had been hit by it with shrapnel. I fell down behind a dirt mound and pulled my pants down to see if I was bleeding even though I had no pain. Not a scratch, I could not believe it, but I pulled up my pants and started firing back at the enemy. Then as quickly as it started, we heard someone yell cease fire. The tank from the rear rolled up and some soldiers ran over to where the enemy had been, but they were gone. So, we continued to our destination, and unloaded the trucks and stayed there that night in tents. I had my boots hanging up off the ground, and as I was laying there about to fall asleep. That is when I saw it, a hole going straight through the heal of my boot from the grenade shrapnel. Another half inch up it would have hit my foot.

On September 13th we loaded trucks up with wounded civilians and headed to our base. No Serbs in site for the whole trip. We heard a lot of explosions and gun fire off in a distance, but we could not see anything from where we were. We got back to our base and I went and got another pair of boots. Went to the motor pool where I saw our Lieutenant was talking to my platoon Sargent about needing this truck to be repaired. I heard the Sargent say that he ordered an oil pan for it last week and it did not come in yet. I kind of walked into the conversation, and I said let me take a look at it. So, I crawled under the truck and saw the oil pan had a bullet hole straight through it close to the bottom, so it could not hold any oil. I crawled back out and said I can fix it sir, Give me a couple hours. He said get it done, so I said I will be back. I went to find Jim; he was an excellent welder. I told him I need your help at the motor pool with something. He was not doing anything at the time, so he said sure. I crawled under the truck and removed the oil pan while he went and got the welder ready. I cleaned the inside of the pan really quick and went out to big scrap pile next to the motor pool and found a flat piece of metal. The welder was also a cutting torch, so after I marked where to cut. Jim cut it to size, then after it cooled some, I cleaned it and filed some of the edges. Put it down into the pan and it stopped snug above the holes, and I said perfect fit. Walked away to get some oil as Jim welded the plate in place. After it cooled down and I cleaned it up, I put it back on truck. Filled it up with oil and went back under the truck to check for leaks. Did not see any so I told Jim to fire it up while I was still under it, so he started up the truck, and still no leaks. About that time the Lieutenant and the Platoon Sargent walked back into the motor pool as I was climbing back out from under the truck. I said we fixed it sir and she is ready to go. Lieutenant said what did you do, so I told him how we fixed it, and

I said its only missing one quart of oil from regular ones. Of course, the pan would have to be removed to change the oil, but it will work. So, he said let me drive it around the base, and I will be back. He came back about 20 minutes later, crawled under the truck and still no leak. He crawled back out and looked at me and said from now on only you work on my truck. So, I said yes sir, as he got back in and drove away. My Platoon Sargent patted me on the back and said nice job soldier.

September 14th came, and it would become one of the worst memories of mine. Some of us were called into the command tent where we were given satellite photos of an area. Now we were not the only people going out on convoys, there were others going to different places, but they were all getting attacked. So, we were told that we were going to an area that a battle had taken place, and we were going to mark everything down on the photo we had. Mark down where everything was found and pick it all up and bring it back on the truck. Apparently, a UN General was going through that area the next day, and they did not want him to see the battle scene. I know what you are thinking; it is a War Zone, there are going to be battle scenes, WAR IS NOT PRETTY. Disgusted with the whole idea of doing this, we ate breakfast and headed out to do our job. We arrived on the field and there was stuff all over the place, so we started splitting up the areas in small groups. Of course, my area had a burnt-up body in it, and I told my group we will do that last, pointing at the body. So, my group split up our area and started to mark down where everything was laying on the map. As we marked down everything's position on our map and walked by it another group was picking each item up and putting it on the truck. There was a lot of brass, (bullet cases), Some weapons, a couple of helmets, and of course the body. After everything was finished in my area, I lit a cigarette and stared at the body, OK maybe two or three cigarettes. There was no smoke coming from the body, but you could smell the burnt flesh. The worst smell you can possibly imagine. I looked at my friend Bob and said do you think it is one of ours or theirs, he said can't tell cause all the clothing was burnt off, and the body looks like ash. The legs were tucked under almost like he was kneeling, and it was kind of turned sideways with one arm bent up like a chicken wing. Half of the body reminded me of burnt wood in a fire that is just ash but still keeping its shape. So, I marked down the position on the map, and called it unknown body. Now this part gets freaky. I handed the map to Bob thinking I was going to grab the chicken wing arm and grab the leg to move it. I hate when my thoughts are correct, as soon as I touched the arm of the body, it fell like ash falling out of a chimney. Half of the body disintegrated into dust, leaving the legs and part of the torso, and some bones. Yeah it freaked me out too, so I had to walk away and smoke a couple more cigarettes. Somebody brought over a shovel and we were able to bag it and get it into the truck. After everyone was finished, we went back to base, where I took a long shower and went the bar. Do not remember much more that night because YES, I got drunk.

September 15th, we went out again on short four-mile convoy taking more stuff to some other town. In our convoy was an open back 5 Ton with medical tanks like oxygen, and those gas tanks like that stuff that explodes. So almost to our destination we were getting shot at again and went for cover. I looked up as I was in my position along with half of my guys, and watched this idiot, I mean lieutenant park this truck right next to us with explosive tanks on it. He ran over and laid down behind cover near us. You could hear bullets ricocheting off the tanks, and I saw red, I mean I was pissed. I stood up and punched the Lieutenant in the mouth, and said you just parked a bomb in front of us. I ran to the truck as I hollered for someone to get the tank behind to move out of the way. I jumped into the truck and put it into reverse as fast as I could; almost running into the tank as it was leaving the road. The whole time I could hear bullets hitting the tanks and sparks when the bullets would hit them. I backed it up enough out of range and stood guard by the truck until our tanks cleared the field of enemy troops. The Lieutenant walked over to the truck just as Captain Nickles was coming over to me, and Captain Nickles said you know

I should write you up for striking an officer. Just then the Lieutenant said wait a minute sir, I was scared and was not thinking. He was rite in getting pissed off, if the shoe were on the other foot, I would have acted the same way. He saved lives by moving that truck away. So, Captain Nickles said if that is how you feel Lieutenant so be it, but Wright don't ever let me see it again. I said yes sir, and he walked away. I looked at the Lieutenant and said sorry I hit you sir, but you scared the hell out of me, and he said me too. We shook hands and got ready to get on our way when I heard someone yell, they got Calvin. Calvin was my friend from the motor pool, and I watched as they drug his dead body up the hill. The rest of the day it was kind of quiet, and I kept thinking to myself I keep losing my friends. I kept thinking how Calvin would always make everyone laugh even if you were having a bad day, kind of jokester.

September 16th, we headed on the longest run I was on, and about 10 miles from our base my truck was hit by a round from an enemy tank. It completely ripped the whole wheel off my truck, and I was on top in my seat. The blast threw me onto the hood of the truck, but as I was falling, I heard that loud high pitch whistle going past my head, yeah bullets. I pulled myself back up towards the seat and saw two bullet holes in the seat where I was sitting. We all went for cover, and it was an all-out battle. We had enemy tanks shelling us, I could see rockets exploding around some of the trucks and around where we were taking cover. In some spots the enemy were only 15 to 20 feet away. It was close quarters combat; I was finding targets and shooting. I know I hit most of the people I aimed at, but I do not know if they lived or died. Well some I know I killed, because you could see the blood splatter as the bullet went through them, and where I hit them, I knew they were dead. Jay and Ed also my friends were in a ditch near mine, and I watched as an enemy tank round hit them directly. Jay was blown to pieces and Ed was blown in half. Everything was like a bad dream; I mean you cannot imagine the devastation of an all-out battle like this. Some movies I have watched come somewhat close, but the real thing is something you cannot recreate. You would have had to have been there to understand, I cannot explain it, it is like the Gates of Hell had opened up and you were battling Satan himself. This was one of the longest battles I had been in against enemy troops, lasting about an hour and half at least. I saw something that day I will never forget; I saw an enemy tank taken out by what we called Tank Killers. This is a multi-exploding bullet that is shot out of an M50. It pierces the armor of the tank leaving a small hole and continues out the other side of the tank with a much bigger hole. It goes through the tank at such high speed that it creates a vacuum inside the tank, to where anything that is not bolted down gets sucked out of the tank. Yeah people too. Leaving the tank empty and can be used by someone else. When the battle was over, the enemy lost all 3 of their tanks and a lot of troops. We lost two trucks and about 8 people, two of them were my close friends that I had worked with since I got to Germany the year before. When we arrived back at our base that night, I found out that 5 of my friends were killed on whatever missions they were on. So, all in a few hours I lost 7 close friends, it is hard to explain how that feels. It just SUCKS.

September 17th, I call my last day. Every day after is just an extra day I have, and I will take as many as I can get. Why do I say that? Well, we were driving through some town where the buildings looked like they were blown to pieces. The walls were half gone and most of the roofs were gone. You could look through the walls and see furniture and stuff scattered all over. I was on the top of the first truck in my seat when I heard a noise like a can or something falling on the right side of the truck. I quickly aimed my M16 towards it, and as soon as I did something inside me said turn around. So, as I was turning around an enemy soldier had already jumped off of a building to my left and tackled me knocking me to the ground with him on top of me, about a 12-foot drop. It knocked the air out of me, and my M16 rite out of my hands. I turned to get up and saw him already on his feet getting ready to shoot me. By this time everyone was shooting and there was a lot of hand to hand combat as well. I knew I was dead. Overall, of the shooting and yelling I heard a loud shot. Thinking I was a Deadman every muscle in my body tensed up to where for a split second I felt my body come off the ground. Then he fell on top of me dead, so I pushed him off and looked, and saw my friend Bob had shot him in the back. So, I grabbed my weapon and jumped up and turned to get back into the fight. As I was turning an enemy Serb hit me with the butt of his gun on the right side of my face shattering my rear bottom tooth. It knocked me to the ground as I could feel pieces of my tooth in my mouth. I hit the ground and tried to spit the tooth out, but I could not spit. I reached up and felt my bottom jaw had been knocked over a couple of inches. I was freaked out and all I could think of doing was getting it back straight, so with all my might I took my left fist and punched myself in the bottom jaw. I have never had so much pain like that in my life. I actually saw stars and I heard a loud almost like a suction cup crunch in my head. At that time, the one who hit me jumped on my back and started chocking me with his AK47. Trust me when I say that there is no two inches of this gun that is smooth. It is almost like being chocked with a sawblade. I tried everything to get him off me, and nothing worked. I took out my knife and started swinging it behind my head, and just when I started feeling weak, I felt the blade hit. I forced it in as hard as I could, and the chocking stopped. I turned and kind of sat up staring into his eyes as he stopped moving all together. I pulled the blade out of his head, but what took a split second seemed like a lifetime. I can still see it like it just happened today. I could feel the blade scrape across his skull, and I watched the whites of his eyes slowly fill with blood. From the time I was knocked to ground from the 5 Ton to this point was only about 3 minutes. I got up and started shooting at the enemy, and I hit one in the knee with the butt of my gun. As he hit the ground, I shot him. Soon this battle ended. The enemy would almost seem like they would vanish, I mean one minute they are all around you and the next you could not find them. Looking around we discovered that three of the UN doctors and one soldier had been killed. I did not know any of them but still I hated losing people.

Klagenfurt
Maribor
Varaždin
Nagykanizsa
Kaposvár
Komló
Pécs
Baja
Subotica
Senta
Kikinda
TIMISOARA
Sombor
Osijek
Novi Sad
Zrenjanin
LJUBLJANA
LUBIANA
ZAGREB
ZAGABRIA
CROAZIA
Kutina
Sisak
Karlovac
Rijeka
HRVATSKA
Slavonski Brod
Vukovar
Vinkovci
BEOGRAD
BELGRADO
Sremska Mitrovica
Šabac
Brčko
Bijeljina
Tuzla
Doboj
Banja Luka
Prijedor
Bihać
Zenica
SARAJEVO
BOSNIA-ERZEGOVINA
Mostar
Zadar
Šibenik
Split
Dubrovnik
Valjevo
Kragujevac
Kruševac
Čačak
Titovo Užice
Novi Pazar
Crna Gora
Nikšić
Podgorica
Kotor
Cetinje
Falconara Marittima
Ancona
Civitanova Marche

We completed our mission and returned to our base.

By the time we returned to our base my jaw was swelled up like I had a baseball in my mouth, and my neck was all cut up from being choked. Captain Nickles saw me and ordered me to go to the medic tent, so I went. Was looked at by one of the medics, and he gave me a bottle of Motrin. That is the Military fix for EVERYTHING, you could lose an arm and they would give you Motrin. He said do not drink on these, and I said no problem. I walked out of the medical tent and saw someone getting ready to walk in, and I gave him the bottle and said take these. Did not know what he was there for, but he will get the same thing, and I headed to the bar. Walked up to the bar and ordered a Bud and a pint of Tequila, turned around and saw Bob reading a letter. So, I took my drinks and headed over to him, and as I walked up, I said what's up brother. He looked up at me and said I'm a dad, as he turned a picture around to show me his daughter. Then he said you look like crap brother, and I told him I would have looked worse if you did not shoot that guy. He had me! He told me that his daughter was only two weeks old and he could not wait to see her. I started pouring shots in some glasses, and I said because of you my son still has a father. We are going to get through this crap, and I will take you there myself, you will see your daughter. We drank that shot, and as I was pouring another. He said that we are getting married in December, will you come with me and be my best man. I gave him his shot and said I would be honored; we drank that whole pint. Jaw stopped hurting by that time, and we stumbled back to the barracks.

The next morning my face was hurting all over, not just in my jaw. Went to try and get something to eat, but I could not chew anything, so I just sipped on coffee. I went to work, and my Platoon Sargent said why don't you go rest up, you look terrible. I said I cannot just sit around doing nothing, working will get my mind off the pain. So, I worked most of my shift, but it did not get my mind off of the pain. My whole face was throbbing so bad I was getting a headache. So, towards the end of the day I walked outside sat down and lit up a cigarette. When I was almost done, I heard trucks coming back from a mission they had been on that day. One that I was supposed to be on, but they took me off because of my jaw. They drove passed the motor pool where I was sitting, and I could see bullet holes in the windows and on the trucks themselves. As they drove passed, I saw my friend Aaron looking at me shaking his head, and he looked like he was crying. I ran up to his truck as he jumped off and he said they are all dead, and I said who. He said Chris, BJ, they hit us hard, Dale, Earl, just everyone. I walked away and saw them taking the bodies of my friends off the first truck, and I just dropped to my knees. The throbbing in my face was completely gone, and I wanted to grab a gun and go hunt these bastards down. People have seen me pissed off but that day I wanted blood! In all I lost 11 friends that day, and all I could think was maybe if I would have been there, I could have saved some of them. I saw Captain Nickles walking over to the tent where they took my dead friends as I was on my knees. I looked at him and said sir don't take me off anymore missions, and he saw my face, I know it was red and he kept walking. My friends and I toasted our fallen brothers, and we all were talking about revenge. We talked about good times we had with our friends we lost but even the funny stuff no one laughed. I do not even think any of us could get drunk.

September 19th another convoy was going out and I was not on the roster to go. I grabbed my gear and headed for the first truck. Walked by Captain Nickles and said sir I am in and continued to climb up to my seat on top of the 5 Ton. He did not say anything to me or try to stop me, so I went. That is the only day I was hoping we would get attack, I wanted to kill that day. We did not see anyone that day, we drove passed the spot where my friends were killed the day before. It was an eerie feeling, and there was a lot of blood on the ground. We completed our mission, and while the truck was being unloaded, I was talking to a Navy Seal that was there. He told me do not look for revenge you will only get yourself killed, just protect each other, that's how you all live through this. I never forgot his words. We got back to our base later in the evening, and by this time I was starving. I had not had anything to eat in a couple of days, so I went to try again. Still could not chew but I could swallow green beans and baked beans, so I ate a lot of that with some coffee. Went to the bar again to drink a couple, but really was not in the mood for it. I went and sat down outside my tent and stared up at the stars for a while, thinking of everything that we had been through, and the people we lost. I was also thinking a lot about my son, and how I could not wait to get home to see him.

September 20th sirens went off early in the morning on our base, so we all came out of tents to see what was going on. The Colonel on the base said gather round men. He said Serbs had taken to the streets in Sarajevo, and they are attacking civilians. We need to take back the streets, so go out there stay safe and let us get this done. Our base was not far from the capitol city, so we did not have to go far to get there. Once we got to the city, we took up defensive positions, and started moving forward looking for the enemy. We were going through the town checking every building and street. When we came across this parking garage, I heard someone yell out, go check it out. I hollered back I got it, and Bob, Jim, Aaron, Raymond, Steve, Cliff, and I went into this big garage. I was walking by this huge concrete pillar when I saw a butt of a rifle being swung at my head. Next thing I knew I was being held against the wall by five of my guys, and Bob was in front of me. At first, he sounded like he was under water and then his words were clear and said are you ok. I said yeah what happened, as my guys let me go. I wanted a cigarette, but I could not move my arms, so I asked Raymond to give me a smoke and lite it for me, I cannot move my arms. So, Bob told me what happened, and I could not believe it. He said you beat that guy to death with your bare hands, as he pointed to a dead Serb on the ground. Then you sat on him and kept punching him in the face and would not stop. We all tried to stop you, and while he was saying all this, I noticed they all had fat lips. He said you were hitting us too when we tried to stop you, hell you threw Jim like a rag doll. Jim said yeah with one arm; Jim was a big guy, body builder type.

I walked over to the dead guy still puffing on my smoke and still could not lift my arms, and I could not believe what I saw. There was no face on this guy, it was just blood and his face was completely smashed in. They all started to pat me on the back saying are you ok now, and I nodded. You could hear some shooting going on somewhere in the city. I could not pick up my M16 because my arms were so worn out by what just happened. So, Bob picked it up and we headed out, and we saw our people walking back to the trucks, and they said it is over. So, we loaded back on the truck and went back to the base. I washed up a little and went to bed, because I was so tired, I could not stand up for long. The next morning, I woke up refreshed and all my buddies were joking with me saying things like we know better than to piss you off. It was funny at first, but I started to think about what made me lose it like that, and I hope I never do that when I go home. It scares me to this day, because I still do not know what my trigger is, if I knew I could protect it and stop myself from going too far.

It was September 21st and we were heading out again, with a convoy. We did not get too far away from our base when a rocket just barely missed my truck and it exploded some trees on the side of the road. We all started running for cover on the side of the road while being shot at, and we were shooting back. All of a sudden enemy tank's came at us, and they were shooting at us too with machine guns and tank shells. One of our tanks were destroyed and on fire, and there were explosions everywhere. I could hear our choppers getting closer, and we were pinned down. I shot everything I could see. I know I hit a bunch of people that day. An enemy tank was getting so close to my position I thought it was going to run me over when all of a sudden it exploded, and I ducked down. I looked up and it was on fire, and I could see our choppers machine gunning all over the ridge on the other side of the street. Our other tank had already destroyed two enemy tanks and was battling another. I kept finding targets and shooting at them, I know I missed some, but I know I hit some too. I saw two enemy soldiers on the other side of the street. One would come up and shoot then go back down, then the other would do the same. I took out a grenade and threw it right at their position, but I thought I overthrew it. Just as it looked like it was going to go passed them, one of them stood up to shoot. The grenade hit him in the face and fell down and exploded killing both of them. This battle was the longest battle I would ever be in while in Sarajevo, it went on like this for almost two hours until the enemy retreated. We lost a bunch of people that day but not from my company, we were all ok. Someone was looking out for us that day. The load we were carrying was mostly destroyed, so we went back to our base. We got back to our base and started unloading the bodies of our fellow soldiers and helping the wounded to the medical tent. The UN personnel were going through the load to see what was salvageable. Later that night there was a ceremony for all our falling soldiers since we arrived in Sarajevo, a lot of them were my close personal friends. They played Taps and Captain Nickles gave a good speech, but I was not really listening. I was thinking about the good times I had with them and I could see each of their faces as plain as day. I still can today. From the time we arrived in Sarajevo to this point I lost twenty friends. I did not want to lose anymore.

September 22 there were no convoys going out. So, a lot of the day was spent getting our gear and weapons cleaned up. Some were writing letters; a lot of cards were played that day. We even had some British and Canadian troops hanging out with us. One Canadian guy told me they had lost thirty-five people, and there were only twelve of them left. I told him, brother if you all want to hang with us, your more than welcome. He told me; I appreciate that Yank, but we are okay. I said I am a Rebel, but that's cool. The British had only lost four, but they only have been on two missions. They were mostly pulling guard duty around base and cooking. We all had a good time that day considering. At the end of the evening Bob and I were sitting outside our tent, passing a bottle of Tequila back and forth. I was telling him about my son and how big he was getting, and he was telling me how he could not wait to hold his little girl. I think about this conversation we had that night often. I still can see the smile on his face when he talked about his daughter.

September 23, we left early in the morning on a 5-mile trip. Things went smooth but the closer we got to our destination the more gun fire we could hear. Where we were going there was a small group of Marines that were pinned down by enemy troops in the town. So, we set up at one end of the town, and started moving forward. We were coming up behind the enemy, and they did not know it, because the Marines were keeping them busy. We started shooting at them when we were about twenty feet away; we all picked targets and shot them. A lot of who we shot at fell, and the rest realizing they were surrounded quickly broke off and left. Once it was a little quieter the Marines came out from their positions and our commanders were talking. Some came over and shook some of our hands, but we unloaded and left to go back to base. When we got back to base, I was told to report to the motor pool. I got to the motor pool, and the Lieutenant that I fixed the oil pan for was waiting for me. I said are you losing oil sir. He said no now they shot my radiator. So, I walked around the whole truck starring at it, and he said what are you doing it is in the front. I said I know sir; I am looking for the sign Please Shoot Me. I said sir I think you should stay on base they seem to have it in for you. He laughed, and said just get it fixed for me, and I said yes sir. So, I took a radiator off a truck that had been destroyed and got it fixed before going to bed.

It was September 24th and we were working in the motor pool when the Captain came in and said grab your gear and let's go. So, we went and loaded up on some hummers and a couple of 5 Tons. On the way we were told the enemy is attacking the other UN base on the other end of Sarajevo. We arrived and saw the enemy outside the base shooting rockets into it. So, we drove closer, and then they started shooting at us. With us shooting at them, and the base shooting at them. Well, let us just say it did not last long, but as they were leaving, they shot a rocket at us. It hit one of the Hummers and destroyed it. The one Captain Nickles was using for cover, and it threw him. Bob and I ran over and said are you okay sir, and he said yeah. So, we helped him up, and went into the base. We saw a lot of damage and some of tents were destroyed with people still in them. We helped some of the people get to the medical tent and helped move some of the bodies too. After a while we went back to our base, and after we ate, we headed to the bar. Captain Nickles was in there already and said I did not think you boys were going to show up. He said what will it be boys, and we kind of looked at each other, then at him, and said Tequila sir. So, he turned around and said give us three to the bar tender. We walked over, and he said I want to thank you boys for coming to me when my truck got hit. We said we wanted to make sure you were okay sir, and he said no one else did. We drank the shot, and he turned to bar tender and said give them another round on me. We said thank you sir, and he turned and walked out.

The next morning September 25th, while eating breakfast, we heard the base sirens going off. So, everyone stopped what they were doing and went outside to see what was up. Someone said a chopper went down, and we got ready to go out on the trucks, to go give support. We went about three miles out and saw the smoke from the downed chopper. As we got closer, we could see it was an Apache Helicopter. There was already a team attempting to reach the chopper, but they were getting shot at by enemy troops. We took up a position on a ridge above the enemy and started firing at them. They shot a rocket at us, but it hit the side of the ridge, and did not hurt any of us. We kept them busy while the team reached the chopper and saved one of the men. The rest were already dead. Later we learned they shot it down with a stinger missile, which is what they shot at us on the ridge.

September 26th, we went on two short missions only about two miles each and we saw no enemy whatsoever. We were relieved to have a couple quiet runs, and the rest of the day we relaxed and played cards. We all were talking about going back to Germany and getting the hell out of there. My buddy Clyde came over and sat down with Bob and I, and just started singing. I heard him sing, I've got dreams, and Bob and I sang, dreams to remember, it is an old Motown song that we all loved. It was starting to get a little late and everyone was getting loud with different conversations when the Platoon Sargent stuck his head in the tent and said we are heading out in the morning. Get some rest.

September 27th, my worst day, like some of them were not bad enough. We left the base heading on a ten-mile trip to deliver some medical supplies and drop off some UN doctors at some town. When we were over half the way there, we were getting attacked again. The enemy had taken up positions on both sides of us, and we were surrounded. There were no good places to take cover, so we were basically sitting ducks. We took cover wherever we could and returned fire shooting in all directions at the enemy. The enemy were so close in some spots, you could spit on them. I had three thirty round clips and used every one of them. It was so chaotic you could not take time to really aim, you just shot in their direction. I watched a lot of people get hit that day on both sides, mostly the Serbs. My M16 was empty and I knew Bob always carried extra clips. He was right next to me behind this dirt mound we had found through all the chaos. So, I hollered over to him, Bob give me a clip, as I was looking for another target. He did not move or say anything, so I tapped him on the arm, and that's when I saw the blood on him. I panicked and sat up while pulling him over to me placing his head on my lap. He had blood all over his face, so I started wiping it off. I could see blood pouring out of his head from a bullet wound, and his eyes were moving like he was trying to look around. His lips were moving like he was trying to speak, but he did not make a sound. I pulled out a field dressing and held it over the bullet hole trying to stop him from bleeding, but there was not anything I could do. His eyes stopped moving and so did his lips, and I knew he was dead. He was the best friend I ever had, and he saved my life just ten days before. I just held him and cried like a baby. You cannot imagine what that feels like and I do not know how to explain it. While I was sitting there crying and holding Bob, my back and head were completely exposed to the enemy. The dirt mound was not good cover in the first place and now I was sitting up. A perfect target for the enemy. Everything was going in slow motion for me and I could not hardly hear anything. I could see dirt flying up next to me as bullets hit the ground, and I could see people in my unit telling me to take cover. I heard bullets whistling passed my head, but nothing hit me. I just sat there crying for probably ten minutes or so. While I was sitting there, I had a calming feeling come over me, and for the first time in my life I believed in GOD. Never gave much thought about God, but like someone would turn on a light switch, I believed without a doubt. When the battle was over people started helping the wounded back onto the truck, and some were looking for any trace of the enemy. Captain Nickles walked over to me with some of my friends, and told me he was sorry, but we need to go. My friends picked up Bob to get him to the truck, and I wiped my eyes and stood up. I felt like I was in a daze, and they helped me into a truck. As we drove by the spot where Bob and I were at, all I saw was blood on the ground. We got back to our base, and everyone in my tent went to bed, I could not sleep. I was looking around and I saw the top of my helmet. It had a brown mark right down the center of cover, where a bullet came so close that it burnt it. I sat up and wrote a letter to Bob's parents about what had happened and laid there trying to sleep. I did not get much sleep that night, but I know I went through a lot of cigarettes, just thinking of Bob and my promise to get him home to see his daughter.

The next morning people were getting up and heading over to get breakfast, they dragged me along, but I did not feel hungry. I went with them and tried to eat but couldn't. My jaw was back to normal now and I could chew, I just did not want to. So, after drinking some coffee I headed back to the tent and grabbed the letter I wrote and took it to the mail tent. I filled out an envelope and gave it to the officer who was sitting there. I then went to the motor pool where I thought I could get my mind off things by working. Let's just say I did not get much done that day. After work I was starving so I got something little to eat, then went back to my tent. I saw the letter I wrote laying on my bunk, so I opened it. Most of what I wrote had black magic marker going through so you could not see what was written on it. I was so mad I just crumbled it up and threw it into the trash. I knew we were not supposed to tell anyone where we were, but I wanted his family to know what happened to him. I swore one day I was going to tell them everything. I went to the bar and drank heavily that evening.

The next couple of days went kind of normal, went to work and laid around the tent in my bunk. Did not really talk much to anyone, just kept to myself thinking of All twenty-one of my friends I lost since we arrived. Someone must have said something to the base Chaplin about me not acting like myself, so he came to my tent to talk to me. I told him I was fine, but he kept asking me questions, so I talked to him for a while. I told him I was sick and tired of losing my friends, and there were too many rules we had to follow but the enemy did not. I told him we should be able to just shoot them on site and not wait for them to kill us first. He said because we are the good guys, and I said then why are we hiding it from everyone that we were there. Then he wanted to talk about Bob, and what he heard I did by sitting up like I was. I told him all thoughts of the enemy left my mind and I just lost it seeing him die. I told him I knew I was being shot at, but I could not move. I felt a calming feeling come over me and that for the first time I honestly believed in God. I said I felt like God was standing behind me blocking the bullets.

October 2nd, my last day going out on any missions. We were teamed up for the first time with another American unit, so it was a lot of people I did not know. We used our trucks with the seats on them, and we were heading out about ten miles to drop off medical equipment to some UN facility. There was a Staff Sergeant with us that was the biggest guy I ever met. Never knew his name because everyone just called him Tank. He was over 300 pounds of muscle, and even the officers called him Tank. Close as I can describe is the guy Coffee from The Green Mile. Well, we only got about a mile away from our base when we were attacked. Everyone was getting into position wherever they could find a spot. Somehow, I found myself next to Tank behind a small ridge with a couple of small trees on it. Looking back at that moment it was like a Monster Truck parked next to a Volkswagen Beatle. We were holding our own and starting to push them back when I heard Tank yell out, I'm hit. I looked over at him and saw him holding his stomach with both hands with blood all over his hands and shirt. I pulled out my field dressings and tied two together, then I tied it around him as tight as I could to stop the bleeding. With everything I had been through up to this point, I cannot begin to explain to you how scared I was, but fear can be a powerful ally. I knew we were only a mile from our base, and I could hear the choppers coming closer to our position. I could not stop Tanks stomach from bleeding, so, I jumped up and picked him up into a fireman's carry over my shoulders. I was 5'9" and 170 lbs., picking this 350 lbs. guy up like he was a sack of potatoes. I started running towards our base, and I knew we were being shot at, I could see dirt flying up next to us and heard some whistle past us. The choppers were flying over us, and I think one came down behind us to give us some cover. I could feel a strong wind behind us, and I could hear bullets tinging off it. I just kept running to the base, and they open the gate as I got close. I ran straight to the medical tent, and they pulled Tank onto a table and started working on him. I turned to go back out, but two doctors stopped me and was pulling my shirt off thinking I had been shot. I was not but I looked like I had laid down in a pool of blood, it was Tanks blood. I was soaked in it from my neck to my feet, and I could feel my clothes sticking to me, and my boots were seeping blood as I walked. By this time, the battle was over, so I headed off to get a shower and a clean uniform. After a while, the convoy retuned to the base after completing the mission. The guys in my unit asked me what happened to me, and I told them. At the same time someone from Tanks unit went to the medical tent to check on him. He came by our tent and asked which one of you carried Tank, and I said I did. He was shocked that I even could, so was I. He told me the doctor said he was going to be ok, but it would take some time.

He said he would have died if I did not get him there when I did, and he shook my hand and thanked me.

October 5th, we were heading back to Germany. Woke up early and we all headed over to get some breakfast. While we were eating the Captain walked into the Mess Hall tent and told everyone we had orders to pack up and go. A new group of soldiers were going to be landing soon to take our place. Everyone started yelling and stomping their feet. We finished eating and went to trade our uniforms back in for our own American uniforms. Once we changed into our uniforms, we went to get our gear packed up and started taking them to a waiting area. We kind of stacked our stuff in piles and we found out we still had a couple of hours before leaving. So, what did we do, Yep, went to the bar. Ran into some of our British and Canadian friends, and we were shaking hands with them and saying goodbye. Had a couple of toasts with them, and we headed out to the flight line. Everyone of us was anxious to get The Hell Out of There. There were a lot of soldiers standing around that I still did not know, but I knew what we all went through. I thought about everything we had been through since we first arrived, and I fell to my knees. With soldiers all around me, for the first time in my life, I prayed to God. I thanked him for getting me through this and told him to take care of my friends that were with him now. Before long we were getting on the plane and taking off. The whole plane erupted in cheers when it lifted off the ground. A couple hours later we landed in France, outside of Paris. Some of the soldiers were stationed there, and the rest boarded other planes to head to our own destinations. That is when it hit us the hardest, looking around seeing how many were not there. I mean we started out with 48 people from Germany, now only 27. The flight was kind of quiet, but we made it back to our home base in Germany. Dropped off our gear and took our weapons back to the Armory. A bunch of us went to the bar on base and got a lot of beers a couple of shots and a lot of PIZZA. I do not know how much I had to drink that night, but I still do not know how I made it back to my bed in the barracks.

October 6th woke up in my bed and I did not want to get up. It had been so long since I slept in my own bed. I did get up though and got cleaned up and dressed. Just as I finished getting dressed my roommate came in and handed me a letter addressed to Bob's mother. My roommate Gary did not go with us to Sarajevo, it was only a few of us in the company that went. Gary worked in the base admin, and he saw all the letters being sent to family members of the ones who died. This one he brought to me, this really made me mad. It was explaining how Bob died in an accident while in Germany and said nothing about combat. I stormed out of the room, and Gary was saying to me to stop and come back in and cool off. I kept walking out of the barracks and headed straight to the admin building. I walked inside and headed straight to Captain Nickles office. Do not think I even reached for the door handle, I just pushed the door wide open and hollered what the hell is this as I was holding up the letter. Captain Nickles and the company First Sargent (Top) were having a meeting, and Top yelled attention, so I jumped to attention. Captain Nickles said I got this Top we will pick up later, so Top left. Captain Nickles walked over to me as he was saying don't you ever come barging in like that. He said I should slap you with an Article 15, which is basically a fine and could result in loss of rank. He closed his door and told me to sit down, so I did and gave him the letter. He said how did you get this, and I said I would rather not tell you, but I think he knew. He told me this is what we had to tell the families, because the United States was not in Sarajevo or any combat. He said the families were getting the full benefits though, but I thought what good is that if they do not know the truth of how their sons died. Then he said I know how close you and Bob were, and that I could go to transport his body to his home. He said remember, we never left Germany is the official statement of the government, but he knew I was going to tell his family the truth. I think that is why he said I could go. He said the plane is leaving in a couple of hours, so go and get packed up. I said thank you sir, and I will be back as soon as he is buried.

I packed a bag and put on my Dress Greens which is the ceremonial uniform of the Army. I arrived at the flight line and told the Colonel who I was, and he pointed to the plane and said their loading it now. So, I started walking towards this C-130 that was being loaded with coffins. I waited till all 10 coffins were aboard and strapped down, and the pilot said find a seat, so I went in. I walked by these coffins with American flags tightened around them. They had name plates on them, so I found Bob's name and sat down on the bench next to him. Once we got into the air, I removed my seat belt and sat on the floor next to Bob's coffin. I flew the whole trip on the floor, just thinking about what I was going to tell his family. Looking at the coffins I had an empty feeling, it was heart breaking. I thought about all the good times we had, and how Bob never saw his daughter in person. After a long trip one of the pilots came back and told me to get back in my seat, we were going to land. We landed at Ft. Meade Md, and the plane drove to one of the hangers. Then the rear of the plane opened, and I got out. There were soldiers there with their Dress Greens on, and they walked into the plane to remove the coffins. As they carried out the coffins one at a time I stood at attention and saluted the whole time. They were taken into the hanger where they were put onto trucks which took them to other planes. There was a Captain there and he said are you Specialist Wright, and I said yes sir. He said Nickles said you were coming in, and he said get in son, as he pointed to Hummer. So, I sat down in the passenger seat as he got into the driver's seat. While driving to the plane I was supposed to get on he told me Nickles was in my class at officers training academy. He is a good man, and I said yes, he is sir. He also told me, that Nickles said that you are a good soldier, as he looked at me and said is that true Specialist, and I said I try to be sir. We pulled up to the plane, and he said it is probably going to be a couple of hours until it leaves, are you hungry. I said no sir, I am ok, thank you for the ride sir, and I got out. He drove away and the truck carrying Bob's coffin pulled up. They loaded him onto the plane and left. I lived in Dundalk, Md and I was so close to home, but I never left the plane. I sat on the ramp of the plane just thinking of everything that had happened in the past month, and how was I going to explain it all to his family. I know I smoked a bunch of cigarettes while waiting to leave. I finally walked over to the one of the hangers and went in to use the bathroom. As I walked out of the hanger, I saw two pilots heading to the plane. One of them saw me and said are you our guy, and I said yes sir. So, he said well let's go, get strapped in and we will get into the air. So, we loaded up and took off. Before I knew it, we were landing on Wright Patterson Airforce Base. I stood next to Bob's coffin as Airforce soldiers in their Dress Blues came onto the plane to get Bob's body. They loaded his coffin into a Hurst, and I walked out of the plane. One of the soldiers pointed to a gate and told me the chow hall is over there. So, I went in and got something to eat.

After eating I was told to go to the headquarters building. There I was told they had a rental car I could use to go to see Bob's family. They told me tomorrow they would bring Bob's coffin to the graveyard. So, I was given directions to get to Bob's house, and I headed out. They were good directions; I drove straight to Bob's house with no problem. I sat in the car a little while smoking cigarettes, and all my ideas of what to say to them were gone. Everything I rehearse on the plane ride over here completely left my mind. Now what was I going to say to them. So, I got out of the car, still in my Dress Greens and walked across the street to his door. I started to knock, and the door flew open, and I heard Dan? I looked and there was Bob's fiancée holding their little girl. I said yes how do you know, and she said Bob sent me a picture of you, and said you were his best friend over there. She let me in, and I saw his parents sitting on the couch. His father said were you there when Bob had his accident. I said yeah, some accident; I looked at his fiancée and said you may want to sit down. As she sat on the chair, I walked over to the fireplace looking at a picture of Bob on the mantle. I said he did not die in no accident, then I turned around to face them. I told them Bob was shot in the head and he died on my lap. I told them where we were, and why we were there. I said he died a HERO, and I told them about the day Bob saved my life. His mother was crying and came over to me and hugged me. I talked to them about some of what went on over there, but mostly of the fun we had in Germany before we went to Sarajevo. I had only one picture of Bob, it was him and I outside our barracks in our BDUs (camo uniform). I took it out of my pocket and handed to his fiancée and said you make sure you tell this little girl her daddy died a HERO. They asked me to stay the night, but I told them I already had a room at a hotel, and I will come back in the morning. I just wanted to be alone. I left and found a hotel nearby and got a room. I went to my room and just fell on the bed and fell asleep. Woke up early the next morning got cleaned up and put my uniform back on. Headed over to Bob's house as they were walking out of the door to go to the graveyard. His father asked me if I wanted to ride with them, and I said no I will follow you as I held up my lit cigarette. So, I followed them to the graveyard, and there were so many cars and people there. He must have known the whole state. His coffin was already in place over the gravesite. Everyone gathered around as a preacher said a sermon, and they lowered his coffin into the ground. I walked over and pulled back the heavy tarp over the dirt mound and grabbed a hand full of dirt and threw it into his grave. I started to walk back to where I was, and everyone started taking turns dropping in dirt. After the ceremony was over, I hugged his family and held his little girl for a second. Then I told them I had to get back. They thanked me for being such a good friend to Bob and for telling them the truth about what really happened. I drove back to the Airforce base dropped off the car and got something to eat. Went to the flight line where a plane was getting ready to head to Frankford Germany.

I slept the whole way over to Germany, and when we landed, I called Captain Nickles and told him I was in Frankford. He said he would send someone to get me. While I waited for someone to pick me up, I got something to eat. My roommate came and picked me up, and we drove back to Wiesbaden. On the way I told him how it went, and I asked him if I got him in trouble about the letter. He said no one said anything to him about it but said do not do that again. We laughed, and he told me not much has been different the past couple of days. I was back to the same routine for a couple of days when I was told I needed to go to the hospital in Frankford. Someone wants to see you, so Sargent Johnson drove me to Frankford. He said he was going to do some shopping and he will be back. He said go to the third floor and its room 305. So, still not knowing who I was seeing I went to the room, knocked on the door, and walked in. As soon as I walked in, I saw Tank; I said Tank, and his mouth dropped. The doctor had just told him a second before I walked in that the soldier that ran with you on his back is coming in. He saw me and could not believe as small as I was, I could run with him on my back. I do not blame him I did it and still do not believe it. His wife was there, and she walked over to me and put her hands on my cheeks and kissed me on the lips and said thank you. We talked a little and then I left. Sargent Johnson picked me up outside and said well how is he. I said he is good he is getting released tomorrow and going back his unit. The following July 1993 I got out of the military. Before I left Germany, I received an Army Achievement Award for what the Captain called it Jerry Rigging the trucks to keep them running. I also received an Army Accommodation Award for carrying Tank when he was shot. Although Captain Nickles admitted it probably would have been a more upgraded medal if we had (actually been there).

I do not know why God showed any interest in me, but I know he saved me. With all of what I went through and all the close calls I had. I only lost my teeth, was never shot, or stabbed; no shrapnel ever hit me. I now have lost all my teeth because of the hit I took on September 17th in my jaw. I do have times where I will hear explosions, or bullets whistling by even though I know it is all in my head. Sometimes I can smell that smell of death, it is a mixture of gunpowder, blood, and burning flesh. I always see my friends faces almost like they are there, and I can hear them talking. These are the kinds of thoughts that drive a lot of VETS to drink, or drugs, or even suicide. Not me, I do not think like that, I see it as one of old friends must be coming to see how I am doing, and I'm good with that. I know God did not see me through all of this because he likes me. So, I try to help people whenever I can, and I try to be a good person. Not to make up for anything I did, because the only regret I have from being in combat was that I did not kill enough of the enemy before they killed my friends. Whatever the reason I was saved, I have one question for God when I reach heaven. It is hard to explain but the way I see God is like when we were kids and would play with a bug. To where you would put your hand down to make the bug go the other way until you guide it to where you want it to go. Well, God does not use his hand, but he puts you in situations or people in your life that make you go the way he intended. Well, I know without a doubt that Bob dying on my lap made me believe in God and walk how he intended me to be. So, my question is this. If I had not been so stubborn in not believing in God, would Bob have had to have died. I will ask him that when I get there, but he will have to wait because I am going to be here for a while yet.

The first year after leaving the military in September 1993, I got a tattoo of an eagle on my chest and gave it a blue eye. Bob liked eagles and he had blue eyes, and even though I do not drink like I used to; I drink two shots of Tequila every September in memory of my friends. I go to karaoke and sing "Some Gave All" by Billy Ray Cyrus and dedicate it to Bob, but it is really to ALL my friends I lost. I have not been able to cry since Bob died on my lap; not even when my mom died, even though that devastated me. I guess that part of me died over there, along with my friends. I raised my two nephews since they were three and four, along with raising my son Daniel. Even though his mother and I were divorced; I think she would agree that I did more then most fathers in that situation. Now that he is an adult and a father himself, I see both of us in him. I could not be prouder. My nephew Robert that I raised is in the Navy and a father himself who I am immensely proud of. I have been through three divorces and now I am married to the love of my life. My wife Barb and I have never said a bad word to each other in seven years together. I do not believe I have PTSD even though she says I fight World War III in my sleep every night, but I do not remember my dreams. In fact, every person that has slept in the same room with me says the same thing. I have woken up a couple times in the past twenty years standing next to the bed in a fighting stance; I look around, do not see anyone and I lay back down, and go back to sleep. I have only two sides; I can be the nicest guy you could ever meet, or I can be the meanest. The mean side I keep locked up inside of me, but if anyone attacks my family or my country, I will release it. I remember the pastor at my church telling me one time that I am too nice. That he could see me starving to death trying to feed someone; I told him you have not seen the other side of me.

Despite what the government says, the story you just read is True. There is not a day that goes by that I do not think about it. I wrote this to share what we went through and the sacrifices of so many good friends. Please honor them and know they died protecting other human beings. They are our HEROES!

I did not do any research on the beginning world events. This is how I remember it.

CPSIA information can be obtained
at www.ICGtesting.com
Printed in the USA
BVHW072025220920
589086BV00006B/189

9 781977 230676